In
CLASSICAL
mood

Air of
Spring

Air of Spring

Springtime brings a feeling of fresh air and new beginnings. This volume strikes a similar chord, with some of the freshest, most uplifting music ever written. There are delightful melodies from Schumann, Delius, Mahler, and Weber. There is Tchaikovsky's glorious *Waltz of the Flowers* and an excerpt from Mozart's famous *Horn Concerto No.4*. There are short, but no less memorable, pieces by Mendelssohn, Grieg, and Schubert, while Vivaldi takes us to Italy, and Delibes transports us to exotic India. And for the finale, there's a magnificent symphonic poem from the Czech composer Smetana.

THE LISTENER'S GUIDE — WHAT THE SYMBOLS MEAN

THE COMPOSERS
Their lives... their loves.. their legacies...

THE MUSIC
Explanation... analysis... interpretation...

THE INSPIRATION
How works of genius came to be written

THE BACKGROUND
People, places, and events linked to the music

Contents

EDVARD GRIEG *1843–1907*

Holberg Suite

OPUS 40: PRÄLUDIUM

he word *präludium* means "prelude"—a beginning, or an opening piece. This Präludium introduces the listener to Edvard Grieg's charming suite. The joyous rhythm on the violins vividly calls to mind spring in his homeland, Norway, where fresh air, wildflowers, and mountain streams bubbling with the cool water from melting snows inspired him.

FOCUSING ON QUALITY

Apart from his famous *Piano Concerto in A Minor* and a symphony in his youth, Edvard Grieg wrote no large concert works. Nearly all of his music takes the form of short pieces and songs, which is why he is often called a "miniaturist." He concentrated on the quality of the piece rather than its length. As a result, his work is beautifully crafted and wonderfully tuneful, with many subtle touches of harmony and rhythm.

NATIONAL FIGURE

Edvard Grieg is not only Norway's greatest composer, he is also a towering figure in his nation's cultural history. Almost everything Grieg wrote reflects the beauty of the mountains and fjords, or echoes the strains of Norwegian folk music and dance, or recalls colorful scenes from Norse history and legend. His most famous works include the *Piano Concerto in A Minor*, two lyric suites for orchestra and for piano, and incidental music for the play *Peer Gynt*, written by fellow Norwegian Henrik Ibsen. Grieg also wrote many lovely songs, nearly all for his wife, Nina, to sing.

Grieg (left) *and a contemporary painting of Bergen, Norway, his hometown.*

LUDWIG HOLBERG

Ludwig Holberg was an 18th-century Norwegian poet and playwright. In 1884, to celebrate the bicentennial of his birth, a statue of him *(right)* was erected in his hometown of Bergen. Grieg, who was also born in Bergen, wrote the *Holberg Suite* as a personal tribute to his fellow countryman mainly in the style of 18th-century Norwegian country dances.

KEY NOTES

Grieg began by writing the Holberg Suite *for the piano only. It was a year before he arranged it for string orchestra.*

FREDERICK DELIUS *1862–1934*

On Hearing the First Cuckoo in Spring

The cuckoo's familiar, two-note call has long been considered a signal of the start of spring. Here, played softly on the clarinet, it steals through the quiet, lush melodies of the strings and woodwinds (flutes, oboes, and bassoons). This is spring at its most poetic: A musical picture of green woods flecked with blossoms, meadows dotted with flowers, and a special sweetness in the air.

SMALL ORCHESTRA

"On Hearing the First Cuckoo in Spring" is the first of a pair of compositions by Frederick Delius entitled *Mood Pictures* for a small orchestra. Its companion piece is the equally lovely and atmospheric "Summer Night on the River."

THE NATURE LOVER

Frederick Delius respected both the power and beauty of nature. As a young man, he was captivated by the swamps and everglades of Florida. Then he fell in love with the mountain air and fjords of Norway, where he became a close friend of the composer Edvard Grieg. Delius also chose to live for much of his life by a river in the small village of Grez, close to the forest of Fontainebleau, in France. His deep love for nature is evident in many of his works, for instance "Over the Hills and Far Away," "Sea Drift," "A Song Before Sunrise," and, of course, "On Hearing the First Cuckoo in Spring."

Above: *A painting of Delius, in his garden in Grez, by his artist wife, Jelka Rosen.*

JELKA DELIUS

No man ever had a more devoted wife than Delius had in Jelka Rosen *(right)*. This talented, German-born artist largely sacrificed her own career to nurse him through his last tragic years, when he was paralyzed and blind. The strain also ruined Jelka's health, yet she insisted on leaving her hospital bed to be with him when he died.

KEY NOTES

The one big city that the otherwise country-loving Delius adored was Paris—so much so, in fact, that it inspired him to write the colorful orchestral piece Paris: The Song of a Great City.

ANTONIO VIVALDI *1678–1741*

The Four Seasons

No.1 IN E, RV269: SPRING

Antonio Vivaldi himself describes his music: "Spring arrives joyously, with bird song and gentle breezes." A storm blows up, but soon passes, and the birds resume their song. In the Second Movement, the solo violin plays a tender and faintly melancholy tune over a murmuring accompaniment, as a shepherd and his faithful dog doze peacefully in a meadow. Finally, peasants dance exuberantly under a bright blue sky, with the solo violin standing out freshly from the rest of the strings. Winter is gone for another year and summer is on its way. The music says it all.

REDISCOVERED TALENT

For nearly two hundred years after Vivaldi's death, the great bulk of his music was all but forgotten. It is only during the last fifty years that scholars and music lovers have rediscovered the enormous extent of his work: the many concertos for stringed instruments; the hundreds of concertos and sonatas for oboe, bassoon, flute, and recorder, among other instruments; the splendid church music; and at least fifty operas. Recently, a Danish scholar, Peter Ryom, catalogued all of Vivaldi's known works. They are now listed with an RV number, the "RV" standing for "Ryom's Verzeichnis der Werke," or "Ryom's Index."

Right: Said to be a portrait of Antonio Vivaldi. Several paintings exist that are supposed to be of Vivaldi, but no one knows for sure what the composer looked like!

CONCERTO GROSSO

Vivaldi's *The Four Seasons* is a group of concertos for strings and solo violin. These concertos are milestones in the history of music because they stand halfway between the older 18th-century *concerto grosso* (great concerto), which divided a string orchestra into a group of large and a group of small instruments, and the concerto as we now know it—a concert work for orchestra and solo instrument.

FELIX MENDELSSOHN *1809–1847*

Songs Without Words

BOOK 5, OPUS 62: SPRING SONG

This is among the best loved of Felix Mendelssohn's many *Songs Without Words* written for the piano. It is thought that his publisher probably added the title "Spring Song" as a very appropriate afterthought. This light, frolicsome piece, with its delicate, tripping phrases, could only have been written about the most uplifting, carefree season—spring.

A SERIES OF SONGS

Mendelssohn published his *Songs Without Words* in eight groups or books, of six pieces each, including two books that were published posthumously.

WORDS IN MUSIC

Mendelssohn wrote forty-eight short piano pieces under the collective title *Songs Without Words* (*Lieder ohne Worte* in German). He composed them for what was, at the time, a fairly new but growing market: amateur pianists who wanted music that was of good quality, yet not too difficult to play in their own homes. Mendelssohn's chosen title perfectly reflects the melodious character of the pieces, which carry individual names relating to the subjects that inspired them. One piece boasts two alternative titles— "Spinning Song" and "The Bee's Wedding"—while several others share the title "Gondola Song."

BACH REVIVED

Mendelssohn, a musical scholar, had a keen interest in the then-neglected works of J.S. Bach and was largely responsible for Bach's mid-19th century revival. In 1829, Mendelssohn conducted a performance of Bach's choral masterpiece *St. Matthew Passion*; this was the first time this music had been heard since Bach's death nearly eighty years before.

KEY NOTES

The little tripping phrases in Spring Song are called "grace notes," or acciaccatura, *which in Italian means* "crushed notes." *Musically, grace notes are used for decoration; in written music, they are printed smaller than the other notes, with a crossed stem.*

ROBERT SCHUMANN *1810–1856*

Symphony No. 1 in B-flat

OPUS 38: FOURTH MOVEMENT (SPRING)

After a jubilant flourish, the main tune comes dancing lightly in on the violins. Other tunes or themes soon grow from it. In the middle section of the movement, there is a call on the horns, almost like an invitation to explore distant woods and fields. This is followed by a brief but enchanting flute solo before the main tune returns. Toward the end, the pace quickens and the music scampers to a finish, its pulse racing with a spring-like zest for life.

OUT OF ORDER

Some symphonies, concertos, sonatas, and other series of works have not been numbered according to their order of composition. In the case of Schumann's four symphonies, the one numbered "4" was actually the second. But he later revised it, which is why it was published as No.4.

A TROUBLED ROMANCE

Schumann's courtship and marriage to Clara Wieck is one of the most famous romances in music history. It also has a dark, troubled side. Clara's father, Friedrich Wieck, was one of Schumann's piano teachers. He predicted a great future for his pupil, but he fiercely opposed the young man's request to marry his daughter: He not only disapproved of Schumann's drinking, he also wanted Clara to become a famous pianist in her own right. For years Friedrich did everything he could to keep Robert and Clara apart. The young Schumann may have been a brilliant pianist, but he was also penniless and far from Wieck's vision of the ideal husband for his delicate and talented young daughter. Schumann later took Wieck to court and obtained permission to marry her, but it had been a long and bitter struggle.

Friedrich Wieck (above) *had no wish to have his pupil as a son-in-law.*

Above: *Clara Wieck and Schumann.* Left: *Leipzig concert hall, known as the Gewandhaus (Cloth Hall), where the Spring Symphony was performed for the first time during a concert in which Clara also played.*

Above: *Schumann at work. During his early years, his composing was remarkably focused.*

CHANGING DIRECTION

Schumann is almost unique among great composers in the way he focused his attention on one kind of music before moving on to another. He began by writing for the piano, resulting in such early masterpieces as "Papillons" ("Butterflies"), "Carnaval," and "Fantasiestücke" ("Fantasy Pieces"). Then in 1840, the year of his marriage to Clara Wieck, he composed nothing but songs—more than a hundred of them. The following year, he changed creative direction again, embarking on the series of symphonies, concertos, and choral works that would keep him busy for the rest of his life— although he also found time to write an opera.

WRITER AND CRITIC

Schumann was almost as interested in writing as he was in music. Some of his compositions, especially those for the piano, are full of references to stories, poems, and names of people and places, almost as though he were writing musical crossword puzzles. But Schumann was also a working journalist: For many years, he edited and wrote articles for the influential German music journal, the *Neue Zeitschrift für Musik (New Music Magazine)*. It was Schumann the music critic who hailed one of Chopin's works with the words: "Hats off gentlemen, a genius!"

KEY NOTES

We know for a fact that Schumann's Symphony No.1 was inspired by the spring, since he gave it the name himself. Later on in life, he abandoned it for some reason, but the name stuck.

FRANZ SCHUBERT *1797–1828*

Schwanengesang

NO.10, D957: DAS FISCHERMÄDCHEN

This love song tells the story of a young man who sees a beautiful girl, "the fisher girl," about to bring her fishing boat ashore and longs to hold her hand. The piano's soft, insistent rhythm hints at lapping waves, while the melody conveys the quickening of the heart associated with spring, the season when new love flourishes.

LIEDER: A SPECIAL KIND OF SONG

Schubert wrote more than six hundred songs, or *lieder*. Some of these compositions, such as "Heidenröslein" ("Wild Rose") and "Ständchen" ("Serenade"), are among the best-loved pieces of music in the world. They combine treasured melodies with piano accompaniments that set off the emotional themes of the songs perfectly. Thanks to Schubert, the German *lied* became a major musical art form.

KEY NOTES

*"Das Fischermädchen" ("The Fisher Girl")
is part of a larger group of songs, known
collectively as Schwanengesang (Swan Song),
which were published shortly after Schubert's
tragically early death.*

13

PYOTR TCHAIKOVSKY
1840–1893

The Nutcracker

WALTZ OF THE FLOWERS

The Nutcracker, a ballet about a child dreaming of her toys, has a Christmas setting. Even so, this glorious, uplifting "Waltz of the Flowers" seems to breathe the very air of spring. After a brief hint of the main melody, there is an elaborate introduction on the harp—much like the unfolding petals of a flower. Then the main theme comes on in full, played first on the horns and answered by solo clarinet. Several other rolling melodies follow before the main theme returns, as the music continues its momentum up to the thrilling end.

EMOTIONAL COMPOSITIONS

Tchaikovsky's music exemplifies the Romantic period in which he lived. Some professionals criticize his work as too sentimental, but this has never affected his wide popularity among his fans.

WORLD OF FANTASY

Tchaikovsky was an extremely emotional man, pouring out his passions and feelings in his symphonies and other big concert works to often devastating effect. His ballets, by contrast, gave Tchaikovsky the chance to retreat into a world of fantasy and make-believe, where his vivid imagination could run free of the cares of everyday life. Perhaps not surprisingly, these inner journeys inspired some of the composer's most captivating music: His *Swan Lake*, *The Sleeping Beauty*, and *The Nutcracker* have long been the three most popular ballets with audiences all over the world.

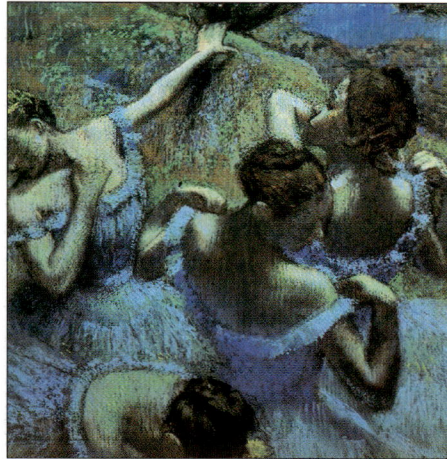

Above: *The French Impressionist painter Dégas shared Tchaikovsky's fascination with the ballet.*

NEW YORK HERALD, WEDNE

MUSIC CROWNED IN ITS NEW HOME.

Brilliant Inauguration of Music Hall by the First Festival Concert.

TSCHAIKOWSKY AND BERLIOZ

The Russian Composer and His "Marche Solennelle" Given a Splendid Greeting and the French Master's "Te Deum" Finely Rendered.

CAMPANINI AND DAMROSCH.

About the Programme, the Performance and the Engagements Indicated

TCHAIKOVSKY VISITS AMERICA

Unlike many of the great composers, Tchaikovsky was famous during his own lifetime. Toward the end of his life he visited the United States. The high point of this visit was on May 5, 1891, when he conducted a performance of his ceremonial *1812 Overture* as part of the opening celebrations for the new Carnegie Concert Hall in New York City.

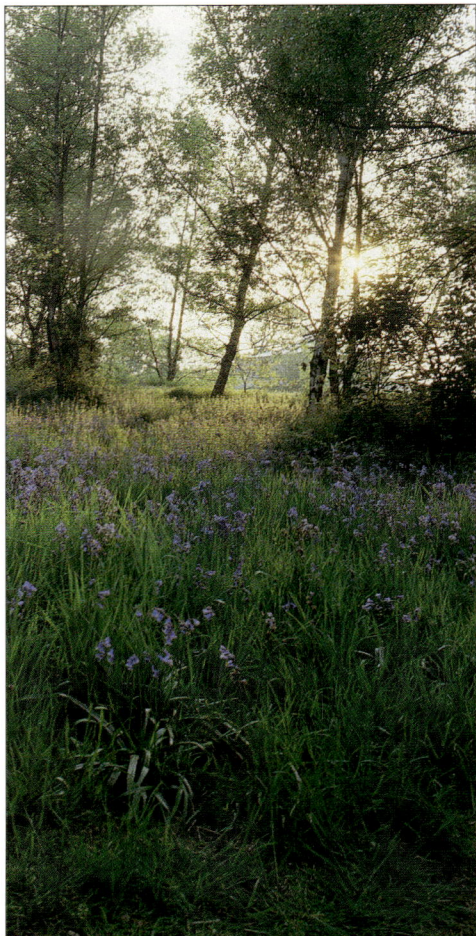

GUSTAV MAHLER *1860–1911*

Symphony No.3 in D Minor

SECOND MOVEMENT

*M*ahler declared: "A symphony must be like the world. It must contain everything." This movement, known by its descriptive title "What the Flowers in the Meadow Tell Me," is indeed written for a very large orchestra, but the composer uses the instruments sparingly, as though to fully enjoy the wonder of each sound. The movement opens with solo oboe playing a simple, peasant-like tune. Violins then enter, making it sound more romantic. Finally there are some rapid, restless passages, as if a sudden breeze were scattering blossoms from the trees, before the piece ends as quietly and peacefully as it began.

WEEKEND COMPOSER

The man who composed ten complex symphonies, plus a massive song-cycle called *The Song of the Earth*, described himself mockingly as "a summertime composer." In fact, this was basically true. For almost all of his working life, Mahler was in charge of an opera house. Only during summer vacations did he have the opportunity to compose. At these times, he retreated to his country home to work in peace on his gigantic projects.

Gustav Mahler photographed in 1907 at the Vienna Court Opera.

VIEWS ON FAITH

In Mahler's Vienna, then the capital of the Austro-Hungarian Empire, most government and other important public offices were open only to Roman Catholics. Mahler was born Jewish, so to secure the coveted post of Director of the Vienna Court Opera, he converted to Catholicism. But there remained a conflict in his mind between the faith he was born into and the one he had adopted for his career. This contributed to the emotional struggles that Mahler expressed with such passion through his music.

KEY NOTES

Mahler called this symphony "my great nature symphony." He titled every movement accordingly. The titles of the remaining movements are: "Pan Awakes: Summer Marches In," "What the Animals in the Wood Tell Me," "What the Night Tells Me," "What the Morning Bells Tell Me," and "What Love Tells Me."

CARL MARIA VON WEBER
1786–1826

Clarinet Concerto No.1 in F Minor

OPUS 73: THIRD MOVEMENT

t is thought that Carl Maria von Weber did not write this clarinet concerto specifically about spring. But the sprightly character of the closing movement certainly has a "spring" in its step, similar to a hare coming out to play after a long winter. The middle becomes more contemplative before the main theme bounces back with spirit.

POPULAR INVITATION

One of Weber's most popular works is his waltz, called *Invitation to the Dance*. The piece begins and ends with the musical image of a gentleman asking a lady for a dance and then escorting her back to her seat at the end of it. Weber wrote the piece for the piano, but other composers—notably Berlioz—also made arrangements of it for the orchestra.

A TRUE ROMANTIC

The German composer Carl Maria von Weber lived at the same time as Beethoven, and his symphonies, concertos, and other instrumental works often have quite a "Beethovenian" ring to them. Weber, though, was first and foremost a composer of vivid operas in the Romantic style. The most famous is *Der Freischütz*, or "The Marksman Who Fires Magic Bullets," which combines a rustic setting with a spine-chilling story of black magic and dealings with the devil. Ill health cut short Weber's promising career in this field, but Wagner later hailed him as the "Father of German Opera."

Weber (left) *and the main characters* (above) *of his opera* Der Freischütz.

VIRTUOSO PLAYER

Weber's works for the clarinet—two concertos and a quintet for clarinet and strings—are among the finest in the clarinet repertory. The man who inspired them was Heinrich Bärmann, principal clarinettist of the Munich Court Orchestra. Bärmann must have been a brilliant player to execute some of Weber's dazzling passages on the clarinets of the day, with their limited keys and stops.

Right: *A clarinet of 1808* (left) *and its modern counterpart* (right).

KEY NOTES

The third movement of this concerto is called a Rondo, which means "round" in Italian. Musically, the term refers to a piece in which the main theme—although other themes intervene—keeps coming around again.

LÉO DELIBES *1836–1891*

Lakmé

FLOWER DUET ("VIENS, MALLIKA")

Lakmé is the daughter of a Brahman—an Indian priest of high birth. In the opening scene of the opera that bears her name, she and her maidservant Mallika are preparing to bathe in the stream that runs through a temple garden. The two women sing sweetly together of the jasmine that blossoms in spring. At the same time, their voices suggest the gentle ripple of water beneath the cool shade of the trees. This is springtime in a very different setting—the mysterious and perfumed land of the Orient.

TWO'S COMPANY

Great solo arias earn most of the applause in opera. But some glorious operatic music has been written for two characters singing together. In addition to the duet between Lakmé and Mallika, there are famous duets for the two fishermen, Nadir and Zurga, in Bizet's *The Pearl Fishers*, for the seducing Don and Zerlina in Mozart's *Don Giovanni*, and for the lovers Rodolfo and Mimi in Puccini's *La Bohème*.

ORIENTALISM IN OPERA

Opera in 19th-century Paris concentrated mostly on spectacle and novelty, and composers were often inspired by exotic places. For instance, in addition to Delibes's *Lakmé*, Meyerbeer based his opera *L'Africaine* on a voyage of exploration to the Indian Ocean, Bizet set *The Pearl Fishers* in the tropical paradise of Ceylon (now Sri Lanka), and the action of Massenet's *Thaïs* takes place by the banks of the Nile River.

Right: *Delibes capitalized on the 19th-century Parisian trend toward Orientalism in the arts* (below).

A BUSY LIFE

The French composer Delibes is best remembered today for his sparkling music to the comic ballet *Coppélia*. But Delibes wrote a great deal of other music for the stage, including his opera *Lakmé* and incidental music to the play *Le Roi s'Amuse*, which is by the great French dramatist and novelist Victor Hugo. Delibes also wrote choral music and songs. In addition to his busy life as a composer, he was also a professor at the Paris Conservatoire de Musique, a government inspector of music in schools, and a church organist.

KEY NOTES

Later in the opera of the same name, Lakmé sings her famous "Bell Song," which tells the story from Hindu mythology of how a girl saves the god Vishnu from harm by playing sweetly on bells.

WOLFGANG AMADEUS MOZART *1756–1791*

Horn Concerto No.4 in E-flat

K495: THIRD MOVEMENT

Riding a horse at full gallop, urged on by the distant horn, is surely one of the most exciting ways to experience the joys of spring. The sprightly, jogging rhythm of this concerto movement suggests such an excursion. One happy tune follows another in this musical canter through the countryside. Near the end, there is a slight pause for breath, before the piece bounds to a finish, leaving the listener breathless, yet refreshed.

Above: *A horn player of Mozart's time used a "natural horn." The extreme simplicity of the instrument made it doubly difficult for soloists.*

THE NATURAL HORN

Mozart wrote this piece for the so-called "natural horn," which was hardly more than a long, coiled, brass tube *(above)*. The absence of valves to alter its playing length meant that the number of notes that could be sounded on the horn was strictly limited, although a skilled player could increase the range by placing a fist inside the open bell end.

BEDŘICH SMETANA *1824–1884*

Má Vlast

VLTAVA

The river in this piece, Vltava (River Moldau), winds its way across Bohemia in what is today the Czech Republic. We hear it starting out as two small streams, the first on the flute, the second on the clarinet. Violins enter with a lovely flowing melody as the streams converge and become a river. The river flows past huntsmen calling to each other on their horns and on past a peasant country dance. It broadens, becoming calm and serene, then hurls itself over rapids before flowing triumphantly through the Bohemian capital of Prague. This "symphonic poem" is a song of praise to a beautiful river in a spring-like land.

FATHER OF CZECH MUSIC

Smetana was a "nationalist" composer, a musical patriot who expressed his love for his country in his compositions. In fact, Smetana devoted his life to creating a Bohemian, today Czech, school of music. His best-known opera, *The Bartered Bride*, is based on Bohemian folk song and dance. His collection of symphonic poems for the orchestra that he brought together under the proud title *Má Vlast* ("My Country") turns to the Bohemian countryside and to his nation's history and legends for inspiration. Like so many past artists, Smetana contracted syphilis and became deaf in 1874. He resigned as a conductor of the Prague Opera, but continued to compose.

It is hard to believe that Smetana composed such life-enhancing work as "Vltava" when he was almost totally deaf. He finally died in a mental asylum in 1884.

Smetana (left), *like Grieg, was a great musical patriot.*

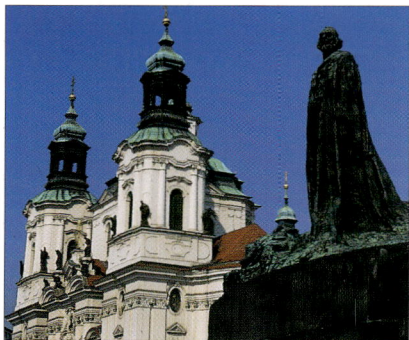

Above: *Statue of Jan Huss, leader of the Hussites, in the town square of Prague.*

MY COUNTRY

"Vltava" is one of the descriptive symphonic poems that make up the song-cycle *Má Vlast*. The others are: "Vyšehrad," the name of the ancient castle that was home to Bohemia's kings; "Šárka," the leader of a legendary band of warrior maidens; "From Bohemia's Fields and Woods," a vivid landscape picture in sound; "Tabor," after the stronghold of the Hussites, a 14th-century religious and patriotic group; and "Blaník," the mountain said to be the final resting place for the spirits of Hussite knights.

CITY OF CULTURE

The Czech capital of Prague, the "City of a Hundred Spires," is famous for its beautiful, historic buildings and for the 14th-century Charles Bridge, which is graced with statues. Prague has also retained its position as a major center of European culture. Every year, it hosts a spring festival featuring folk songs and dances, along with the music of Smetana and his two great compatriots, Dvořák and Janáček.

Prague by twilight, with the Charles Bridge in the middle of the picture. Culturally, it is one of the richest cities in Europe.

MY LIFE

Smetana subtitled another of his works, the *String Quartet No.1 in E Minor*, "From My Life," which is like a musical autobiography. In the last of the quartet's four movements, the composer interrupts the flow of the music with a long, high note on the violin. This high E is thought to represent the whistling in Smetana's ears that signaled his approaching deafness.

KEY NOTES

A symphonic poem is an orchestral composition with a program—in other words, the music either narrates a story or evokes a particular scene or mood.

Credits & Acknowledgments

PICTURE CREDITS

Cover /Title and Contents Page/ IBC: Images Colour Library

AKG: 3(cl), 7(bl), 10, 11(t) (cr), 24 (bl)
Bridgeman Art Library, London/Towneley Hall Art Gallery & Museum, Burnley: 4;
Christie's London: 6;
John Noott Galleries: 8; Rafael Valls Gallery, London: 13; Pushkin Museum, Moscow: 15;
Roy Miles Fine Paintings, London: 20; The Fine Art Society, London: 21(bl); Museum Fur Geschichte die Stadt Leipzig: 22 (r); Victoria and Albert Museum, London: 23
Britstock-IFA/C.L.Schmit: 2; Roger Cracknell: 16;
E.T.Archive: 3(bl), 9(bl);

Hulton Deutsch: 3(r), 21(c);
The Image Bank/ Castenada: 24 (r)
Images Colour Library: 25
Lebrecht Collection: 5(bc), 11(bc), 11(tr), 11(bl), 12(r) (tl), 17(c) (tl), 19(tr), 19(c);
NHPA/Silvestris: 18;
Performing Arts Library/Curzon: 14;
Royal College Of Music: 5(tr);
Tony Stone Images: 9(tr);
Topham Picture Point: 7(tr).

All illustrations and symbols: John See